FRIENDship MATTERS

David Spriggs
& Darrell Jackson

SCRIPTURE UNION

Scripture Union, 207–209 Queensway, Bletchley, MK2 2EB, England.

© David Spriggs and Darrell Jackson 1999

First published 1999

ISBN 1 85999 229 3

All rights reserved. No part of this publication may be reproduced, stored in a retrieval system, or transmitted, in any form or by any means, electronic, mechanical, photocopying, recording or otherwise, without the prior permission of Scripture Union.

The right of David Spriggs and Darrell Jackson to be identified as authors of this work has been asserted by them in accordance with the Copyright, Designs and Patents Act 1988.

British Library Cataloguing-in-Publication Data
A catalogue record for this book is available from the British Library.

Cover design by David Lund.
Printed and bound in Great Britain by Cox & Wyman, Reading, Berkshire.

CONTENTS

Preface   5

Introduction   7

1 Why friendship matters   11

2 Friendships count   19

3 Case studies   27

4 Bible tour   35

5 Improving your friendships   45

6 Friendship talks   55

7 Danger!   61

8 On the way   71

PREFACE

Pamela was still only a young woman, but already she had had a husband who was a pimp, been divorced, started another long-term relationship, suffered several miscarriages, been raped and then got caught up in prostitution as well as Hari Krishna. She was desperate and, in her words, 'about to take the tablets to end it all'. How could God help someone like her?

The answer was surprisingly simple – through friendship. A girl who sometimes looked after Pamela's children (yes, she had those too!) invited her to a coffee bar at the church across the road. There she met a 'middle-class woman' who, much to her surprise, had a similar story to Pamela's. In a few weeks, this woman was able to assure Pamela of acceptance and support not only from herself but also from Jesus. Pamela found this friendship to be real and, although she still has a lot to sort out, she is gradually making it! Such is the gospel power in Christian friendship.

This series, 'Relating Good News', is intended to help us maximise the opportunities for evangelism in our relationships and to become more relational people. Today, quality relationships have proved to be the most effective way of winning people to Christ. Jesus himself understood the value of good relationships for his ministry, as did Paul – someone who knew well how important it was to 'become all things to all people so that some may believe'. We too must recognise that, in an age when 'the medium is the message', the quality of our relationships will greatly affect our ability to communicate an adequate gospel.

Not all our friendships will be intense and long-lasting (think of the babysitter's role in Pamela's life), yet we can learn how to make the most of the brief encounters, too. The books in this series, therefore, are about equipping us to be effective in sharing God's good news within the whole variety of relationships we may have. If you want to be better at relating, if you long to see your relationships honour Christ, if you desire to see the people you know become friends of Christ, my prayer is that here you will find much to help you as you seek to share your faith as well as your friendship.

David Spriggs

INTRODUCTION

Welcome to Philippi, gateway to Europe, first-class advert for imperial Rome, commercial power house – and, for Christians, a danger zone.

Paul and Silas arrived a few days ago, full of divinely driven expectations. A man had appealed to them to come from Asia to help the people of Macedonia (where Philippi was located). He seemed friendly enough, so they accepted his invitation and went. They took their time to get the feel of the place, then friendships started to blossom.

Pre-eminently, there was Lydia – a real class act. A woman on her own, she had developed her business in quality cloth and was doing amazingly well for herself. She was the first to respond wholeheartedly to God's offer of friendship in Christ. She already believed in God, in a general kind of way, but when she heard about Jesus that was it – there was no stopping her or her entourage. It was a very encouraging start, especially as she provided Paul and his group with 4-star accommodation in her own home for as long as they needed it.

Then things started to go wrong. Paul and Silas found they had exchanged 4-star treatment for multi-stripe cruelty. They wound up in the stocks, their bodies bruised and bleeding from the vicious beating they had been given. Instead of the caring attention of Lydia's household, they now had the scorn of hardened criminals to add to their misery. They

Friendship matters

were, humanly speaking, powerless and totally vulnerable.

What had gone wrong? A slave girl – a fortune teller – had pursued them relentlessly for many days, shouting out after them in the street. She had spoken the truth in one sense, because she recognised that they were servants of the Most High God, but her reputation turned it all into a mockery. In the end, Paul had confronted the evil spirit which was the source of her insight. Unfortunately, she and it were also the source of money-making for her masters. They became angry when she lost her occult abilities and vented their wrath on Paul and Silas, claiming they were troublemakers. Hence the death-row accommodation the pair found themselves in.

What next? Pain, hunger, death? No, the unexpected. As Paul and Silas prayed and praised (the other inmates must have thought they were mad!) there was a fearsome shaking. Chains clattered to the floor. The prison doors collapsed. The way to freedom was theirs.

Half-awake, the jailer struggled to his senses. Fearing that the prisoners had escaped, he prepared to kill himself. Just in time Paul intervened: 'Do yourself no harm. We are all still here.'

Within half an hour the tide had turned. The jailer took Paul and Silas into his home. The earthquake had shaken more than the prison: it had shattered this campaign-hardened veteran. He had scarcely stopped trembling with fear before he was trembling with excitement. When he and his family heard about Jesus, they were overwhelmed with joy and became believers. After all, they had seen so much of his love demonstrated in that one act of kindness which had prevented the jailer's self-destruction. Paul and Silas could have been angry and vindictive, but instead they offered forgiveness and generosity. Deep friendship took over where inhuman and unjust punishment had gone before. Friendship – human and divine – won the day.

Introduction

When Paul and Silas met the others in Lydia's house the next afternoon, how they revelled in the account of what God had been doing. Everyone had thought they were dead and gone forever. But now there was that special sweetness of an unanticipated meeting with someone precious, like a reunion of long lost friends.

You can read this story for yourself in Acts 16:9–40. As you do so, keep your eye on the friendship aspect. While there was no single continuous relationship behind these conversions, friendship is the medium through which the approach to offer the gospel was made. All kinds of people became Christians through friendship, from a wealthy woman with an interest in religion to the over-dutiful jailer. Their networks of social and family contacts were powerfully influenced too, and in different ways: whilst one person responded in a prayerful context, for another it was signs and wonders that prepared the way. But all needed a friend to tell them the story.

In this passage from Acts, we find compressed into a few verses events which may have taken weeks in reality. Their story shows the impact of concern, sensitivity, commitment, forgiveness, giving and receiving, shared experiences, joys and sorrows, all of which form the basis of friendships, short or long. They show how God can work with people like us, through ordinary and extraordinary happenings, to reveal his Son to others as we live out our relationships. We may not have to endure beatings and earthquakes as Paul and Silas did, yet we can experience the satisfaction of seeing people we relate to on a day-to-day basis drawn to the Good News of Jesus. Helping us to do this, or do it better, is the purpose of this book.

The first chapter begins by exploring how and why friendship matters in evangelism. The next three chapters explore how friendship works, drawing on real-life stories, case studies and biblical experience. Each chapter contains sections to help you stop, think, engage with the material individually or as a group, and apply the insights to your own situation. The following chapters look at how we can become better friends and some dangers to watch out for. The final chapter is aimed at helping you get on with the job. This book, then, is not intended to be 'an enjoyable read' (although I hope it is that!), but rather to help us bring our relationships into the light of God's presence and allow him to work through us for the benefit of our friends.

When Paul saw the need in Philippi, he took the risk of going with the Good News. Perhaps you see the same need in your friends and family. It is my hope that this book will be your ship to take you to them with that most precious gift of all – friendship with God through Jesus Christ. The encouraging news for us is that the evidence shows that our relationships, particularly our friendships, can make a vital contribution to almost anyone coming to faith in Jesus Christ. Perhaps the time will come when, like Lydia and Co, you too will enjoy recounting the story of how God used your relationships to bring others into his kingdom.

Chapter 1

WHY FRIENDSHIP MATTERS

> The plans were carefully worked out and included a nostalgic drive, the perfect dinner out, low lights, mood music, and finally the question. Everything went wrong ... [nothing] went according to plan – except that the question got asked.
> The answer floored him. It was yes! Then she explained; 'I said yes not because of tonight but because of the last year. For all the times you gave me ... yourself – your time, your love, your overwhelming concern, your desire to see me become a better ... me.'
> *(Arthur McPhee, Friendship Evangelism, Kingsway, 1980)*

Powerful stuff! Well, romantic anyway, and certainly a cameo of the persuasive power of friendship to bring about life-shaping decisions. Of course, the question was not 'Will you accept Jesus Christ into your life as Saviour and Lord?' but 'Will you marry me?', yet many of the dynamics are the same. Certainly, Arthur McPhee must have thought so when he included this quotation in his book *Friendship Evangelism*. Although many things have changed in the last twenty years, today more than ever Christians are extolling the virtue and even the necessity of friendship, or relational, evangelism.

Why has friendship evangelism become so important? It is partly because we have been learning some lessons over the last ten years. In that time there has been a monumental focus on evangelism: much has been written, much has been done, and what seems to have come out on top is 'friendship'. So while it is true that you can now take a Masters degree in Evangelism, it is also true that each of us can make the vital contribution of our friendship without going anywhere near a university!

I suppose it was John Finney who first told us what we already knew, that friendship was a key ingredient in many people's acceptance of the gospel. Finney examined accounts of how over 500 adults came to faith. They varied in their ages, social and geographical backgrounds and their church allegiance. 'One of the most important parts of the research was to find out what people saw as important in their becoming a Christian. We were well aware that the most important factor is the work of God, but what means does the Holy Spirit use?' (*Finding Faith Today*, Bible Society, 1992). People were asked two questions: (1) what was the main factor, and (2) what were the supporting factors in their coming to faith?*

So, what did Finney discover? That about 60% of people placed a quality personal relationship as the number one factor in bringing them to faith in Christ, and almost 30% would add this as a secondary supporting factor. These statistics show that friendship is the most effective evangelism tool around.

This is an exciting discovery. It means that there is no limit to who can contribute. We can even conceive that evangelism might be enjoyable: we can spend time with people we like, doing things we like! It also means that we have a serious responsibility, because if we are not seeing our friends and family members come to faith we should probably be doing something about it.

Even before John Finney's research, Lesslie Newbigin had been saying something similar, although not perhaps so simply. Newbigin spent much of his life as a bishop in South India, working in a multicultural, pluralistic society (as ours is increasingly becoming). One of his discoveries, borne out of his experience, was that 'the church is the hermeneutic of the gospel'. In other words, if anyone wants to make sense of the gospel they need to look at the Christian community, for it is here that we see the gospel being lived out. This is both an amazing privilege and an awesome responsibility. The Christian faith is not a set of mathematical formulae: it takes flesh and blood to communicate it (John 1:14). And it is the church (the Body of Christ) which conveys the truth about Jesus, not any one person. However, we as individual Christians need to play our part in helping others to make sense of our faith, through our relationships with them.

In his down-to-earth book, *Sowing, Reaping, Keeping* (Crossways Books, 1995), Laurence Singlehurst writes:

> What are the basic things that people need to know? I believe that they need to start with understanding certain characteristics of God, such as: God is good; he is alive; he has not just wound up the universe and left it. They also need to know that Christians are all right; are not a bunch of fundamentalist maniacs; and that we are not hypocrites.

Otherwise, we are setting ourselves the Herculean task of inviting people to join something that is, to them, fairly unattractive: to commit themselves to a monster (ie their picture of God), and to turn into an alien (someone religious, boring and sub-human, ie their picture of a Christian)! Who in their right mind would want that? However, through our friendships we can start to change others' perspectives and therefore their understanding of what being a Christian is all about. Incidentally, Singlehurst claims that after hundreds of surveys among Christians, he generally found that 70% put friendship as their number one factor for becoming a Christian.

Alpha is generally recognised to be one of the most effective evangelism programmes today. It includes an instructive video or audiotapes, runs very professional training courses and has insightful written materials. But at its heart is friendship. Most people are invited through a friend. Once there they are offered friendship in all kinds of ways: through the meal, which they may share with the friend who brought them; through the presentation, which adopts a warm, vulnerable, story-based style; through the informal groups, where openness, honesty, acceptance, understanding, listening and response to personal needs are all encouraged; through the day or weekend away, when there are more meals together and social events; and, finally, through the celebration of people coming to faith. Throughout the programme a relational environment is encouraged, in which to foster friendships.

Probably the most effective 'Crusade style' evangelist operating in Europe at the moment is Luis Palau. It is now standard practice in the huge missions run by his organisation to promote, through their literature and training, the necessity for friendship evangelism. The December 1996 issue of *There's More to Life – Update* led with a feature on 'Friends for Life', which states, 'Statistics show that by far the most effective way of bringing people to the Lord is through Christian friends sharing their faith.'

So there you have it. Christian friendship, properly used, is a very effective way to evangelise. Why is this? There are two reasons: (1) because of our culture, and (2) because of the content of the gospel message.

Our culture

We all know that our culture is changing and changing very rapidly in many respects. Over the last twenty years there

Why friendship matters

have been significant shifts in our attitudes and lifestyle, all of which can be summed up by the phrase 'post-modernism'. Here are some of them:

- *Food:* fast-food outlets, convenience foods, microwaves.
- *Entertainment:* television, blockbuster movies, multiplex cinemas.
- *Work:* computers rule OK, short-term contracts, flexitime, job shares.
- *Values:* Living together, gay liberation, equal opportunities, pluralism, alternative medicines, the New Age.

These developments have led to a fundamental change in our attitude to truth. People are more concerned about whether something works rather than whether it is true. There is almost total scepticism about the value of rational argument: what matters is the spin doctors' skill or media image. We cannot expect to discern immediately whether what appears convincing is in fact correct. We need to trust someone before we will accept that their message is authentic, and we need to see that message proved over time before we will accept that it is truly important. The idea of life-long commitment to a person or ideal is considered strange, and needs to be modelled and experienced before it is given credibility. Something may suit you but not suit me; but the more I appreciate you, the more I am likely to think that what suits you may well suit me, and at least I should try it. All of these features and factors somehow get covered through a valid friendship relationship.

Naturally, people can have all these and not be convinced about Christian truth or converted to Christ. But if unbelievers do not experience the friendship of Christians, it is less

Gospel content

> In the past, God spoke to our ancestors many times and in many ways through the prophets, but in these last days he has spoken to us through his Son ... He reflects the brightness of God's glory and is the exact likeness of God's own being...
>
> *Hebrews 1:1–2*

In this passage from Hebrews, and in many other passages in the New Testament, there are indications that the spoken or written word – and perhaps, by implication, any logical presentation of the gospel – cannot be adequate. The gospel cannot be reduced to a formula, however fine and refined.

> Through [God] Christ changed us from enemies into his friends and gave us the task of making others his friends also. Our message is that God was making the whole human race his friends through Christ.
>
> *2 Corinthians 5:18–19*

This succinct comment, from Paul's letter to the Christians in Corinth, reveals that the gospel is relational in content, means and outcome. If this is the case, then we can see that friendship is a powerful vehicle for evangelism because of the very nature of the gospel itself. The Good News is about a changed relationship; it requires a relationship which has the power to change us and the way we relate to God; and it is communicated through people. This raises issues that we will examine more carefully later, but at the very least we can see how the friend and the evangelist are often synonymous.

User-friendly recap
The quick trip to Philippi via the introduction showed us three key truths about friendship evangelism:

- God is able to bring all kinds of people into a living relationship with himself through Jesus.
- How people come into relationship with God varies enormously.
- Friendship seems to be something God chooses to use in many of those journeys to faith.

In other words, the Bible shows us that our friendships, whether they be very deep or quite superficial, can play a special part in helping people come to Christ.

Change has been a significant feature of society in our time and, if anything, the value of our friendships has increased. Statistics show how important relationships are when people become Christians. When we think about successful programmes like Alpha, we soon see that friendship is very much involved in their success.

Note
* For further information, see also *Journeys into Faith*, Bible Society, 1993, pp40–41.

Chapter 2

FRIENDSHIPS COUNT

'Friendship', said Christopher Robin, 'is a very comforting thing to have.'

A A Milne

Let me introduce you to some real people.

Dave, Gillian and Ray

Dave was shaking as he put the phone down – whether with excitement or with fear, he couldn't be sure. He suspected that it was a mixture of both. The phone call had come out of the blue. He hadn't spoken to Ray for several months – not because of any ill feeling between them; there just hadn't been any need. True, the last time he had seen Ray, Dave had said to give him a ring when he needed to. And, he remembered, he had prayed for Ray from time to time. Even so, he hadn't expected this.

Ray was operations manager at the Cable TV station. This was what had brought them into contact on and off for about a year. Dave had come to respect Ray. He was fairly tough in negotiations, but he was also positively helpful. During the months they had been thrown together he had grown to like Ray, and he thought Ray probably liked him too. But, until now, he had felt it was just business and the occasional drink together.

Now Ray was on the phone, talking to him about his

Friendship matters

wife's needs. Gillian, it seemed, had developed ME. In a few short months, from being a physically active person enjoying a full-time job as PA to a dynamic executive, she had dwindled to spending all day on the settee and then having to drag herself upstairs at the end of the day. Doctors seemed unable to provide help or hope. Ray was willing to try anything. Remembering that Dave was into spiritual things, he had phoned to ask him what he thought about faith healing.

Dave went over in his mind what he had said. He had warned Ray about getting involved in Spiritualist meetings, if that was what he meant by faith healing. (Dave's own church had a team who prayed with people for God's healing.) He had also said something about healing being what God wanted, and that it was more to do with God than our own feelings or hopes. Anyway, in the end Ray had said, 'Why don't you call and talk to Gillian? Come any time.'

So when he was out their way, Dave did just that. Ray was out, which meant he had to wait while Gillian struggled to get to the door. She made him very welcome, but he still felt a bit uncomfortable. He listened as she told him about the course of her illness. Then he explained how, in the New Testament, Jesus had healed people, and that his church was discovering that Jesus sometimes did the same today when people asked God for healing. Presumably this was how he ended up praying for Gillian. Dave didn't feel that he had any faith – he kept thinking he was probably getting it all wrong – but he didn't have much choice. Something in Gillian was responding to God. As he drove away, he wondered what Ray would make of it all.

He didn't have long to wait. The next day Ray phoned to thank Dave for calling round. He was sure Gillian was already improving; he asked him to please go round again. Dave called a few more times every couple of weeks. Gillian became more and more excited about God. Dave encouraged her, as she was resting, to invite God to be with her and to heal her. It was beginning to make a difference: she was aware of God's love for her, and hope was returning to her and Ray.

Dave thought it was now time to bring others on board. He introduced Gillian and Ray to a retired couple who were members of the church's 'prayer for healing' team. They visited Gillian and prayed with her on a regular basis. Within six months her improvement was quite remarkable. Physically, she was about 80% back to normal; emotionally, her original brightness was noticeable; spiritually, she was coming alive. She was reading the Bible and listening to Christian tapes. And she and Ray started coming to church.

Within a few months Gillian and Ray both made a clear Christian commitment. It was a special joy to Dave when he saw them expressing their commitment through baptism. As they recounted their journey to faith, he was astounded to hear that it had all begun because, at work, Ray had found him trustworthy and a little different; something in Dave had attracted him. Then Dave had let him know that he was a Christian. When the crisis built up for Gillian, all these things had prompted Ray to call him. Dave had never expected that their friendship would count for so much.

Rosemary, Pete and their neighbour

Pete and Rosemary seemed to have everything going for them. They had a lovely young family, full of energy and demanding, of course, but with no obvious extra problems. Pete had a stressful job, like many of their friends; but he found it fulfilling, and it provided them with an adequate income. They had a pleasant home, many friends and even got on well with their neighbours. Apparently all was well.

Then, over a period of weeks and months, imperceptibly at first, then with increasing intensity and regularity, clouds of depression rolled in. Rosemary began to find it difficult to cope. Tiredness became her dominant experience – even going to the shops became a struggle. She felt useless and hopeless.

Pete was as supportive as he could be, but in some ways this made Rosemary feel even more guilty. What was worst of all, however, was how she felt about God. 'I'm supposed to be a Christian,' she told first herself and then Pete. 'What good am I? What kind of witness is this?' Her faith, which should have supported her during this time in the emotional desert, only added to her sense of total despair.

Then one day a neighbour asked if she could call in. 'Why not?' Rosemary thought. In fact this friendly lady was always coming round to help – with the children, the shopping and, eventually, even the cleaning. Rosemary regarded her, rather ironically, as a 'God-send', but felt that it was she who should have been helping her neighbour, not the other way round!

When the neighbour came, however, Rosemary got a surprise – she had come not to offer help but to ask for it. Rosemary couldn't believe it. The lady wanted to know how she could have a faith like Rosemary's! She explained it like this.

Over the last few months she had seen with increasing clarity the hell Rosemary was going through. The closer she got to Rosemary, the more a puzzle began to form in her mind. Why should Rosemary go on believing in God? The more she struggled with this, the more she could come up with only one answer: God must exist and he must be worth knowing. Rosemary's faith was not for comfort or convenience – she was getting precious little of either. Rosemary was persisting in her faith because God was really there.

Rosemary couldn't believe that they were having this conversation and that God could work through her in this way. Soon, however, she had the satisfaction (joy would be too strong a word for her emotional state) of knowing that her neighbour had become a Christian and thus her sister in Christ.

Roger and Carol, Graham and Jane

Roger usually kept his eyes open for any new faces at church. It wasn't always easy with 400 in the congregation, but somehow this new couple found him. They did not approach him or anything like that, but it was as though God's spotlight was shining on them.

There was nothing particularly exceptional about them – average dress, average number of children (in practice, the nearest anyone can get to 2.4 is 2!), average people. However, Roger made sure that he said hello at the end of the service.

It was the same when they came back a few weeks later, only this time Roger said how pleased he was to see them again. So, over a few months, the beginnings of a friendship formed. Roger sensed that the couple, Graham and Jane, were lonely and in some ways bewildered by all that was going on. After a few months he felt it was right to broach this issue. He asked them what they thought of the church now that they had come a few times. Graham and Jane replied that they liked it but found it 'a bit big'. Roger took this as his cue. Would they like to drop in for a coffee or chat? Or would they prefer him to call on them? They could get to know each other better, and he could explain a bit more about the church. They opted for the latter 'because of the children'. Roger fixed a time and said that his wife, Carol, would come along too.

After the first visit Roger felt very positive about the way the friendship was developing. Graham and Jane had shared a lot about themselves and their family. Carol had been able to tell them the story of how she had become a Christian. She was involved in a training process which was helping her to see that building bridges of friendship was a natural 'way in' to sharing her own experience of Jesus and the general message of the gospel. She was also discovering how to help new Christians own their personal commitment and start the process of discipleship. All this made Roger much more confident when he and Carol made their return visit.

However, in the event, he was soon feeling that his confidence was unfounded! Right from the start everything went wrong. To start with, Graham was going to be late home. Then just as they were getting going on their conversation, one of the children was sick. Once that was sorted out, the phone rang: it was Jane's mother. Why didn't she think to say, 'Ring me back', Roger wondered as the conversation dragged on for twenty minutes. At last they were settling down again – and Graham arrived home tired and hungry. Was it all worth it?

A few visits later the couple's interest in Christian things continued unabated. Jane and Graham were coming to church frequently now, so Roger invited them to a special dinner the church was arranging, when a well-known evangelist would be interviewed about what being a Christian really meant. Graham was pleased to be able to take Jane out for an evening: they didn't have many opportunities with their young family. He was particularly pleased when Roger said reliable baby-sitters were part of the deal.

Roger prayed like mad and worried endlessly about what might prevent them from coming. But on the night they turned up, enjoyed the dinner and the chat-show-style presentation of the gospel, and they accepted the invitation to respond. In fact, it turned out that a few weeks earlier they had followed Carol's explanation of how to respond to Jesus and were looking for a cringe-free way of telling people. The dinner event was just what they needed.

Roger and Carol are still their friends. Graham and Jane are still growing in their faith and service.

We can all appreciate stories like these; probably we have all heard similar stories. But is it really that easy? (Actually, few of the people involved in the events above would have described them as easy – more like 'blood, toil, tears and sweat'!) Can our friendships come to matter so much to others? Do we need to be special before our friendships will contribute significantly to people coming to faith? Are these journeys the exception or the rule? We will explore these questions in the next chapter.

For further reflection

1 Can you spot any similarities and any differences in these three stories? You may find it helpful to think about where and how the friendships took place; what factors turned them into an opportunity to present the gospel; whether anything else was a necessary part of the journey to faith.

2 Did friendship play a significant part in your becoming a Christian? If so, what kind of relationships were involved, eg a school friend or work colleague, a neighbour, a church member, someone who shared a hobby, a family member? Were they occasional or long-standing relationships?

3 From the Christian viewpoint, are there any potential dangers in these stories? Think, for instance, of how things could have gone wrong and what might have happened.

4 How many friends do you have who are not overt Christians? Imagine what a difference it would make if they became Christians through your friendship with them.

Chapter 3

CASE STUDIES

The biblical mandate for relational evangelism is found in the great commission (Matthew 28:19–20). Jesus passes on to us what was given to him by his heavenly Father. Just as the Father sent the Son to befriend lost humanity and extend to them his offer of eternal life, Jesus sends us to do the same (John 20:21). In this chapter we will be looking at some typical ways in which Christians today might do this.

Through community activities
Graham
'Life hasn't been all that easy for me. For a start, I did not have a very helpful childhood. Dad was emotionally distant and severe. Mum was very involved in the family confectionery business. As an only child I was something of a loner, and grew into an adult who found it difficult to make relationships.

'Joining the army didn't really match up to Dad's expectations for me, and even though I married and had two lovely daughters, he never gave me any sign that he was pleased with the way things were going. I found it hard to believe that anything I did would ever come to very much. I left the army, and eventually the marriage fell apart – another failed relationship – and alcohol became an ever closer companion.

'The feeling that I was supposed to do something useful with my life was as strong as ever (thanks to Dad) and I joined the local community action group. There I met Steve and Sally. I soon found out that they were Christians. Through what they said at the meetings, it was clear that they really cared for people in our town. They were always good company for me when the group members met together in the pub after the meetings.

'I don't think we talked about religion until I bumped into Steve in the street. After we'd been talking a while, I asked if I could go round to see him at their house, to ask a few questions. He seemed happy enough for me to do this, and that was the first step I took towards becoming a Christian.

'I know that it was God who was at work in my life, but if it hadn't been for the friendship of Steve and Sally, I don't think I'd be here to share my story with you.'

For further reflection

1 Imagine that you are Graham. What aspects of the friendship offered by Steve and Sally, both to each other and to you, would you consider important?

2 What do you think are the main things Graham is likely to be looking for in such a friendship? What emotional as well as spiritual support do you imagine he will have? What would you feel if you were Graham?

3 What support would Graham need from the church (members and leaders) to help him develop effective evangelistic friendships with the other members of the community action group?

Group activity

How many of your group are or have been members of community organisations? Did you find it easy or difficult to build friendships with non-Christians? List the difficulties. As a group, work together to find practical ways to overcome those difficulties.

Case studies

Through the workplace
Alan

'The first that my boss, Eric, knew about my church connection was when I had to explain that 16 December was no good for the office party because I was already involved in a Christmas concert arranged by our local church. I look back today and wish that I'd been a bit more up-front about my faith at an earlier stage. However, things worked out in the end.

'Eric didn't seem too surprised when I told him about the Christmas concert. In fact, he later told me that it suddenly made sense of a lot of things. He'd often wondered what it was about me that marked me out from the other employees. True, I could be "awkward" at times. For instance, I consistently refused to fob off customers and suppliers with half-truths. This had infuriated Eric at first, but I had firmly but politely told him, "If I'm not being truthful with them, how do you know I'm not going to treat you and the firm in the same way?" Eric conceded that I had a point and eventually came to see this as one of my strengths. The business world is a place where few people can be completely trusted.

'Over time Eric had come to value me, not quite as a friend, but certainly as an asset to the business and as a colleague. As a result he was more than happy, after they had arranged the office party for 17 December, to consider taking up my invitation to attend the church Christmas musical. Eric and his wife enjoyed it so much, they decided to go to the Christmas services. At the end of the service they took home a leaflet with details of the enquirer's classes. In mid January, they joined one.

'The rest, as they say, is history and I was thrilled to take part in their joint baptism.'

Friendship matters

For further reflection

1 In the workplace, are there differences in forming friendships with (a) your peers; (b) people in authority over you; (c) people over whom you have authority?

2 Encourage members of the group to talk about the value they place on friendships like those mentioned in question 1. How do they feel about those friendships?

Group activity

1 Brainstorm answers to the following questions, writing them up on a large sheet of paper. When you have finished, decide together on some practical ways in which you can carry one of them forward.

- How might your church help you bridge the gap between church and the workplace more effectively?

- What opportunities are there, other than at Christmas, for Christians to introduce friends to evangelistic events?

Is there anything on your list that you feel would be most worthwhile organising as a church activity? Talk with the leaders of your church about your chosen suggestion.

2 How important is maintaining an uncompromising ethical stance alongside our attempts to befriend work colleagues? Do you have any experiences where you have been faced with dilemmas like Eric's? Share your stories of success – and failure!

Cross-cultural friendships
Cathy and Deepah

This case study is written as a dialogue so as to allow two group members to take part in a role-play. Role plays often encourage insights to emerge that might otherwise be missed.

Cathy: I first got to know Deepah as a teenager, while I was doing a week's work experience with a social worker in Birmingham. Her parents had moved to the UK from Bangladesh, and they were in contact with the social worker for a reason which I've now forgotten.

Deepah: Cathy was the first white friend of my own age I'd ever had. In fact she is probably still the only white person I would really describe as a friend.

Cathy: Deepah was the first Asian Muslim I had got to know. Her culture fascinated me and I was keen to learn more about her family's customs and practices.

Deepah: Cathy was so helpful to me. My culture dictated that I should marry at an early age, and in my late teens I was introduced to the man who was to be my husband. Being born in Britain, I felt confused. I felt both Western and Asian. Cathy helped me to keep in touch with the things about Western culture that I valued and which I feared I would lose hold of as I got to know a very honourable, though very Asian husband.

Cathy: One of the things Deepah taught me was that there was no divide in her life between the secular and the religious. She talked readily about the religious dimension to life and here we found a meeting point. It helped me understand some of the positive things about Islam, but it also made me appreciate my own faith more. I'm pleased that she has not become so Westernised that she has lost this outlook.

Friendship matters

Deepah: Cathy helped me to understand that being white and being a Christian were not automatically the same thing. I still struggle with this a little bit – it seems to go against the grain for me. My husband is a devout Muslim but I'm interested in these things too. I think that Cathy's God shines through her. She really cares.

Cathy: I was really pleased that Deepah asked me for help when her marriage hit a few difficult patches. My phone bill rocketed during those few months! I think she values my advice and I'm pleased about that.

Deepah: I sometimes wonder whether Cathy's God and mine are the same.

For further reflection

1 What are the pitfalls to avoid in this kind of cross-cultural situation?

2 What particular factors would Cathy have needed to bear in mind because Deepah is a Muslim?

3 What has been positive about their friendship?

4 This friendship has existed for nearly fifteen years now. Are there any further steps Cathy could take to make her Christian witness even more effective?

Group activity

It would be worth contacting one of the Christian organisations working amongst Muslim communities in Britain, and asking if they have a representative who can talk about this kind of work. You don't have to be an Asian to talk to Asians!

Family and friends
Martin

'My wife, Helen, became a Christian several years ago. It wasn't something that was expected, and although I believe she's sincere when she tells me how it all happened, I find it very hard to swallow. Apparently what happened is that she was out walking with the dog on the local moorland and, she says, she met with Jesus. I agree that it made a major difference to her life. She started attending the local church and became a member there after she was baptised. I found the service very moving, although I wasn't really sure why. It was great that Helen had found something important in her life, but I didn't really need anything like that.

'As the managing director of my own medium-sized business, there aren't many things I don't have. I brought my company through the recession. I'm a survivor. Mind you, I had a slight shock when a couple of years ago I had a heart attack. I was really surprised when members of the church came to see me in hospital. I'd always hovered around the fringes of the church, usually going on special occasions, for Helen's sake. I'd got to know a few of the men – not well, but it was they who visited me in hospital. It was totally unexpected, but at least they were practising what they preached – that impressed me a lot.

'The church ran an Alpha group and one of the business men from the church, who I had got to know quite well after he visited me in hospital, invited me to go. I went along because I think the church sees me as a fairly strong-minded and argumentative type – ideal for this Alpha group, my friend told me. I found the groups really genuine. At least I got all my questions in. The group didn't come up with any totally satisfactory answers, but at least the people there were genuine – that impressed me. I'm still open to persuasion though. I guess I'm just your typical agnostic!'

Friendship matters

For further reflection

1 What qualities do you think are required of a Christian when witnessing to members of their family?

2 How has the church family supported Helen in her ongoing witness to Martin? What additional help could they give?

3 What other types of 'events' suitable for agnostics might be arranged by the church to move people like Martin further along the road to faith?

Group activity

What are the sorrows and pain of sharing your faith with family members? Do any of the group members have stories of success to share? What can be learnt from these? What can be learnt from our failures? Discuss ways in which you could support each other.

Chapter 4

BIBLE TOUR

Now that we have reflected on some contemporary examples of quality relationships that have contributed to peoples' faith journeys, in this chapter we will look at examples from the Bible. Here, too, we will find help and encouragement to value our relationships as a medium for evangelism. We start our biblical tour with the greatest evangelist and friend of all, Jesus himself.

Jesus enjoyed the company of his disciples – they weren't there simply for him to practise his teaching style on. Above all else, they were his friends. As they got to know Jesus, they got to know God. Jesus showed them what God was like. The Incarnation – God becoming a human being in Jesus of Nazareth – is at the heart of everything we believe about relational evangelism. It shows us that God desires real and personal relationships with human beings. It is our prime motivation for building friendships with those who need to hear about and see the love God has for them.

Jesus makes friends
John 4:1–26; Luke 10:38–42; 19:1–10; Mark 2:13–17.

For personal study
1 Select one of the Bible passages listed above.

Friendship matters

2 Imagine that you are the person Jesus approaches in your chosen passage. Run through the encounter in your mind. What things do you think would have struck you about him? Think about the way he spoke, the things he said, his looks, his mannerisms, his behaviour.

What was it about Jesus that persuaded you he wanted to befriend you?

For group study

1 Invite each group member to choose a different passage, then spend ten minutes thinking about the questions outlined in 2 above.

2 Invite the group to imagine themselves as these people meeting in the local market. Encourage them to start up a conversation about their encounter with Jesus. They will want to mention the different (or similar) ways in which he befriended each of them.

Comparing friendships

Using the chart opposite, explore the different ways in which Jesus struck up conversations and allowed these to develop into friendship.

Some tough questions:

1 Why is it unusual for Christians today to have conversations with people who are on the margins of society, like the woman from Samaria?

2 What support does a Christian need when trying to witness to colleagues who are involved in fraudulent or dishonest work practices?

3 What kind of people might be considered 'tax collectors and sinners' in today's society?

	Luke 10:38–42	Luke 19:1–10	John 4:1–26	Mark 2:13–17
Who started the conversation?				
What requests did Jesus make?				
What kind of person did Jesus befriend?				
How much time did Jesus give to developing the friendship?				
In what ways was the person changed when Jesus befriended him/her?				

Friendship matters

Ananias makes friends with Paul
Read Acts 9:10–19; 22:12–16.

Something to think about
Who was the most influential person in your early Christian life. What did you learn from him/her? What kind of a person was he/she? How did God use that person to help you grow and develop as a young Christian?

If you are studying this passage as a group, people might like to share memories of those who shaped their early Christian lives.

Ananias: a man with a mission
Ananias had a frightening job to do. A vicious opponent of Christianity had apparently made a complete turn around, and God had chosen Ananias to be his first Christian friend. To do this required a special kind of person, and Ananias seems to have fitted the bill. What was it about him (the person he was, the things he did) that made him stand out as an ideal person to nurture Paul in his new faith?

Working your way through the two Bible passages, list as many of Ananias' qualities and actions as you can.

Bible passage	Ananias' qualities	Ananias' actions
Eg Acts 9:10	He was open to God	He obeyed God

Bible tour

Friendships for life

We don't make friends with people just so that we can 'get them saved': we should have an ongoing commitment to them. However, our friendships will develop in especially precious ways if our friends do become Christians. The way that Ananias helped Paul is a clear reminder to us of the importance of giving support to someone during the early days of their Christian life.

1 Starting with the list you have drawn up for Ananias, write down all those things that would help you to get alongside and make friends with a new Christian (eg encouragement).

• *Encouragement*	•	•
•	•	•
•	•	•
•	•	•
•	•	•

2 Think of the pressures that new Christians are going to face. How will your friendship equip them to cope?

3 If you have been a Christian for a while, you may be able to remember people you helped at an early stage of their Christian life. Is there anything you would have done differently? Imagine the difference it would make if your recently converted friend went on to become the next Billy Graham!

4 Complete the following sentence, 'One thing that I can learn from Ananias, and from the way he befriended Paul, is…

Paul makes friends with Onesimus
Read through Paul's letter to Philemon (all of it! Don't panic; it's only one chapter).

Hello, Paul! Hello, Onesimus!
Imagine the conversation between Paul and Onesimus, from the moment Onesimus knocked on Paul's door. What might Onesimus have offered as the reason for his asking such a favour from Paul? How do you imagine Paul reacted?

Optional exercise: Act out the conversation on the doorstep in pairs, one of you taking the part of Onesimus, the other the part of Paul.

Exploring deeper
1 Philemon 6: Paul says that those who share their faith with others experience a fuller understanding of everything Christ has done for them. Have you experienced anything like this? If you have ever experienced hostility from non-Christians as you tried to share your faith, how did you feel? Did the Holy Spirit seem more real at such times?

2 Philemon 10: To what event in Onesimus' life is Paul referring when he says, 'who became my son while I was in chains' (v 10, NIV)? If Onesimus was not a Christian before he found Paul in Rome, why do you think he looked Paul up? How do you imagine Paul befriended Onesimus before helping him come to faith in Jesus?

3 Philemon 9: Love is essential to Paul's relationships with his converts and co-workers. What practical forms might this love have taken?

4 *Philemon 12:* Paul says that sending Onesimus back to Philemon will be like losing a part of himself. What is it about new Christians that can be so encouraging to those who have been in the faith a long time?

5 *Philemon 13:* How soon does your church encourage new Christians to get involved in evangelism? How often have you heard it said that new Christians need thorough discipling first? Think about the number of non-Christian friends you had before you were converted (if it is possible to remember) and the number you have now. How can your church encourage new Christians to get involved in evangelism?

Making friends with people from different backgrounds

1 List the social, ethnic and other differences between Paul and Onesimus. Why do you think Paul was able to overcome these differences?

2 Read Galatians 3:26–28. What does this tell us about Paul's view of the Christian family?

3 Complete the sentence: 'As a result of what I have discovered in this Bible study I will…'

Cheerio, Paul! Cheerio, Onesimus!

Imagine the conversation between Paul and Onesimus as Onesimus left to return to Philemon. What might they have said to each other? What might Onesimus have thanked Paul for? What might Paul have thanked Onesimus for?

Optional exercise: Act out the conversation on the doorstep in pairs, one of you taking the part of Onesimus, the other the part of Paul.

Friendship matters

Peter makes friends with Cornelius

We sometimes forget that Jesus' first followers were Jewish. It's hard for us to understand how difficult it was for Jews to take their good news about Jesus to non-Jews (Gentiles). In the early chapters of Acts, Luke records how surprised the Jewish disciples were at the way the Holy Spirit touched the hearts and lives of Gentiles. Imagine how you would feel if your church asked you to take responsibility for evangelism in a predominantly Muslim area of a large nearby city or town. Peter probably felt just as awkward and fearful as you might as you begin to make the first contacts with your Muslim neighbours.

Read Acts 10:9–33 (you may also like to read 10:1–8 and 10:34–48).

1 List the things about this chapter which surprise you.

2 List the things that encourage you.

3 List the things that confuse you.

Group exercise

If you are studying this passage as a group, compare what you have written. There may be others in the group who can help you with the confusing bits!

Historical note - Hospitality laws for Jews living among Gentiles: In Acts 10:23,48, Luke records the fact that Peter provided hospitality for, and received hospitality from, non-Jews (Gentiles). Verse 14 helps us to see the importance Peter gave to observing the Old Testament laws. Jews had very strict laws about entertaining and being entertained by Gentiles. In verse 15, God makes it clear that helping to bring others to faith in his Son is so important that there are no cultural or religious boundaries which we cannot cross in order to befriend people.

For discussion:

1 Make a list of the different social, national, chronological or cultural factors that apply to the people who attend your church. If possible, attempt a similar exercise for your village, town or city district. Compare the two lists. Are there any significant groups from your community who are not represented in your church family?

2 What is the challenge of Acts 10:34–35 for your church situation?

For further reflection

Read through the Bible passage carefully and answer the following questions.

1 What should I believe?

2 What should I reject as false or untrue?

3 What do I need to change about my witness to others? How can I change it?

Note

Over the last few years a group of people, who could be described as 'God-fearing' (see Acts 10:2, NIV), have gradually come to understand that what they used to believe about the Christian faith was wrong in several important areas. Now the churches known as the Worldwide Church of God have made important amendments to their former beliefs. Gradually, they seem to be developing a more fully biblical understanding of Christian faith.

There are many people in other non-Christian cults and sects who are genuinely seeking the truth. Sadly, most are led astray by systems of teaching that are far from biblical, yet they will often be willing to talk with you about spiritual things. Think about the Jehovah's Witnesses. Next time

Friendship matters

they call, why not invite them back for a further visit and then, in the meantime, ask one of the leaders in your church to join you for a Bible study with them? Contact one of the many Christian agencies who offer help to Christians trying to witness to cult members.

NB: Don't try to talk to such people alone. They are usually well prepared and will readily confuse you with their repetitive arguments. However, considerable numbers of former cult members come to faith in Christ each year.

Final exercise:
1 Think about the kinds of young people who hang round the local town centre. Note any features of their lifestyles about which you disapprove.

2 Spend time in prayer, asking God to show you which of these are due to your different cultural values. Do you need to say sorry for judgemental attitudes over some of these things? How, in the future, are you going to see them as God sees them? Ask God for opportunities to cross the cultural barriers.

Chapter 5

IMPROVING YOUR FRIENDSHIPS

User-friendly recap
Having explored how and why friendship can contribute to evangelism, we looked at some contemporary situations. Chapter 2 introduced us to three real sets of people who have all seen God work through friendship. Dave was asked for help through a friendship formed in the workplace. Rosemary showed how God can use our weakness to bring our friends to himself. Roger operated as a friendly person within the church culture.

Chapter 3 contained case studies on friendship evangelism, illustrating the different dynamics that can exist within a friendship.

Chapter 4 was a survey of biblical material from the New Testament, looking at friendships formed by Jesus, Paul and Peter.

Improving your contacts
It is important to note that when we talk about friendship evangelism, we do mean *friendship*. However, friendship is a very broad category and different people have different definitions. Here are a few perspectives on friends and friendship:

> **friend** *n.* **1** a person with whom one enjoys mutual affection and regard. **2** a sympathizer,

> helper, or patron. **3** a person who is not an enemy or who is on the same side.
>
> Fate chooses your relations, you choose your friends.
>
> Jacques Delille
>
> Two are better than one,...
> If one falls down,
>   his friend can help him up.
>
> Ecclesiastes 4:9–10

But however we view it, friendship means something about genuineness, valuing the other person, wanting to be with them for their own sake, liking them, sharing an interest or an activity with them. So, when we talk about increasing our friendship contacts for 'the sake of the gospel', we need to be careful that we don't mislead or offend people. Remarks like 'I'm giving up working with the youth group because I want to spend more time making new friends, to win them for Christ' or 'The gym's a great place to build relationships for sharing the gospel' or 'Our church is telling us to go down the pub so we can make more friends as part of our evangelism strategy' may easily be misunderstood. Superficially, it sounds as though our friendship is solely a means to an end. That would be to cheapen friendship and, in fact, we would cease to be real friends at all.

Friendship evangelism is far more than just a strategy. There is the implicit recognition that friendship is a fundamental characteristic of our faith. Jesus' whole ministry was focused on friendship: he was known as 'the friend of sinners'; he came to turn us into God's friends. Understanding the dynamics of the friendship God offers in Christ should enrich our human friendships. Further, whenever there is valid human friendship, people are living in a parable of God's desired relationship with us. Thus friendship is valuable in itself because it is a taste of the fullness of the gospel.

To debase it, cheapen it or prostitute it is to debase the gospel. Therefore Christians have a very high stake in maintaining a proper understanding of friendship.

The other reason we need to seek out more friendships is because not having them means that we are probably failing in our discipleship. It is important to remember that *we* need friends, not to improve our discipleship performance rating, but because having friends and being a good friend are valuable things in their own right. We need the friendship of other Christians to maintain our spiritual well-being, our effectiveness in Christian ministry and our ability to cope as we live out our faith. But it is just as necessary, and as much fun, to have non-Christian friends. We need friends, we need a number of them, and we need to offer them appropriate levels of friendship.

The best way to move forward is not to set up targets for how many friends you should have and then try to hit them. Rather, simply plan to make yourself available in the right places and at the right times. You may indeed have to give up the youth group, go to the gym or the pub or, as Steve and Sally did, get involved in a community group. Difficult decisions may have to be faced, which may affect fellow-workers in the church or family members. A circle of Christian friends – who enjoy going to the theatre, stock car racing or eating together – should be willing to break up their circle and invite non-Christian friends to these occasions. Alternatively, they could split up so as to release each other for quality friendship with people outside the church.

How do you decide with whom to develop friendships? Clearly, this must be a constant issue for prayer. Continually offer yourself to God and be open to people he brings you into contact with at work, during your leisure time, in your neighbourhood. As you do this, some of those relationships will develop, or you will find that there is more opportunity to spend time with certain people, as happened for Dave with Ray and Gillian. You may find that particular individuals start to come to mind more frequently and that this prompts you to pray for them. Soon a relationship, which previously had been distant or cool, becomes closer and warmer. In other words, God starts to bless some relationships more than others. This is a good indication that he wants you to deepen your friendship with those people. Naturally, you need to keep in touch with God concerning these relationships, thank him for them, ask him whether the way things are going is right and discern from him what the next step might be. You may discover that others are far better placed to help your new friend and that your task is simply to serve as the bridge.

A word of warning here. Once God is in charge of your friendships, there may be some surprises. He may offer you friendships you never anticipated! Alan was surprised when he and his boss Eric became friends. So try not to rule anyone out. Equally, don't assume that everyone with a need who crosses your path is meant to become an intimate friend, or you will end up totally exhausted and probably without any proper friends at all.

It is also vital to bear in mind that what matters most is the *quality* of the friendship we offer, and this is closely related to the Christlikeness of the person God has mysteriously been growing in each of us. People who have experienced deep, quality friendships will bring a richness to the most momentary meetings; whereas those who can only relate superficially will struggle to convey trust, affirmation, enjoyment and commitment, however much time and energy they invest in a relationship. There is something here about a transparency which cannot be faked but can only grow. (I suspect that this was part of what appealed to Rosemary's neighbour.) Nevertheless, we can all develop skills to enhance most of our friendships. We will touch on some of these now.

Improving your friendship skills

1 Think for a moment about each of your friends. What qualities do they have which attract you to them? (Draw up your list before going on to the next section.)

Name	Attractive characteristics

2 Your list is likely to include the following:

- Able to really listen to me, empathise, is interested in my opinions, respects my viewpoint.
- A good conversationalist, shares experiences, expresses feelings and opinions openly.
- Appreciative of things I do and say, makes me feel needed.
- Is fun to be with, humorous, enjoys the same things as I do, willing to do what I want, widens my understanding and activities, not too pushy.
- Is helpful, generous, sensitive, reliable, trustworthy, available when I need him/her.

Friendship matters

- Is not always doing the talking, insisting on his/her own way, is not dominating, dismissive.
- Won't let me down; doesn't make me feel that she/he only wants me for what she/he can get.
- Is not always dependant on me.

Probably, your friends will find positive characteristics in you too: that's what attracts them to you and keeps the friendship going. (You may wish to re-read the true-life stories and case studies in earlier chapters, and note the characteristics implied there.) From your list (and ours), you will see that friendship, in addition to the mysterious factors, involves skills – listening skills, communication skills, relational skills. All these can be improved once we become aware of our deficiencies – as long as we desire to change. As Christians, we have additional motivation (to be more like Jesus) and additional resources (especially the Holy Spirit who is growing the fruit of the Spirit in us).

3 How can you set about improving your friendship skills? One practical way is to find a small group of Christian friends who will covenant with you to seek, with God's help, to grow into better quality friends. You will all need to agree:

- To be gentle and honest with one another.
- To support and encourage one another.
- To spend time sharing your strengths with others where they are weak.
- To meet regularly and to pray for one another daily.

Having made this commitment, make a list, for each member of the group, of the personal qualities you find helpful

Improving your friendships

(eg six features; call this list 'STRENGTHS') and a list of personal qualities you find unhelpful (eg three features; call this list 'WEAKNESSES'), in terms of friendship. Thus if there are four people in the group, each person will have three other people's view of them. It will work better if it is a group you can trust, where you have already formed good relationships. Otherwise, it may feel threatening to have strengths and weaknesses pointed out! Sharing this kind of experience can deepen friendships significantly.

Take the three views and, together, identify common strengths and weaknesses. Then, in turn, share insights about how, with God's help, you can each grow out of your weakness. Others in the group may be able to share their own experience of how they coped with a similar weakness. Try to be as practical as possible about a plan to re-train each other. So, for instance, if someone finds it hard to make conversation, others in the group who are better at it can share how they do it. Of course, this may not be easy if a skill comes naturally, but please try. Here are some examples:

'Well, I remember particular things, so that I have something to say.'

'I'm always working out what might interest them.'

'Before I meet up, I think of four experiences I could relate.'

'I always want to know what's been happening to the other person, so I often ask questions.'

'I have trained myself to become more aware of my feelings and to be less fearful about sharing those feelings with others; and I try to find the words to express feelings.'

You may all agree to look out for weaknesses and alert group members to them – but make sure you are also watching out for progress and affirming this too! You may also all agree to help someone improve. (This is probably easier for conversational skills than, say, being humorous or generous; although those who have problems with the latter could be asked to bring the cream cakes next time the group meets!) It is important that each member has the opportunity to share times when they feel they have made progress as well as occasions when they feel they have failed.

It is also vital that everyone feels supported throughout and that each group member takes seriously the need to pray for the others. Thank God for progress, ask the Holy Spirit to continue to make you more like Jesus, and seek for forgiveness. However, try to avoid becoming so self-conscious that you cease to function naturally. Please encourage one another, because this sort of change is hard work. Like Jesus, we need to keep our eyes on the joy ahead of us (being a better person and friend, which will please God) as we endure the difficulties.

Perhaps your circumstances – for example, your work or family commitments – prevent you from meeting with others as a group. If you cannot get together because of problems with time, it is well worth re-adjusting your lifestyle so that you do have a few hours free each week to spend with others. If, however, the problem is that you have no Christian friends to meet with, then perhaps working through one or more of the following books will help. They all offer insights and practical help to move us towards the kinds of change that will make us better friends:

Friends and Friendship, by Jerry and Nary White, Navpress, 1987.

A Bible Study on Friends and Friendship, Navpress, 1983.

The Measure of a Man, by Gene A Getz, Regal Books, 1979.

The Measure of a Woman, by Gene A Getz, Regal Books, 1978.

Jim Peterson, who has written several books around the area of friendship and evangelism, comments that non-Christians 'generally decide either to accept or reject Christianity according to what [they have] seen'. At first this sounds rather onerous; it certainly underlines the need for genuine, quality friendships. But before you panic too much and feel that you don't have enough to give, please note the following story.

For four years Jim regularly held one-to-one Bible studies with a very intellectual Brazilian called Mario. It was high-powered stuff. Eventually, Mario became a Christian. A couple of years later they were chatting, and Mario said to Jim, 'Do you know what it was that made me decide to become a Christian?' Jim immediately thought of all those high-powered Bible studies. But it turned out that it had been something much more ordinary. Jim had invited Mario round to share a bowl of soup with his family. During the meal the children had behaved badly and needed correcting, something which had frustrated Jim at the time. But Mario had seen things differently:

> 'As I sat there observing you, your wife, your children, and how you related to each other, I asked myself, When will I have a relationship like this with my fiancée? When I realised the answer was "never", I concluded I had to become a Christian for the sake of my own survival.'
>
> Living Proof, *Jim Peterson*, © 1981. Used by permission of NavPress Publishing Group. For copies call 1-800-366-7788.

We should not underestimate the value of Jim's integrity nor the impact of all those years of exposure to the scriptures. However, in the end it was not what Jim regarded as his strengths but the weakness of his family which drew Mario to a decision. So don't be discouraged. While it is important to be the best kind of friend we can possibly be, in the end God is well able to take our weakness and foolishness, and to use them within our friendships to draw others into his perfect friendship. When God is at work in the lives of others, it seems that they can become blind to our faults as God's Spirit focuses them on what is Christlike in us. Perhaps we should even pray that this will happen!

Chapter 6

FRIENDSHIP TALKS

> Be ready at all times to answer anyone who asks
> you to explain the hope you have in you...
> *1 Peter 3:15*

'It's good to talk,' says BT, and most people would agree. So why is it that when Christians dream of speaking to their non-Christian friends about their faith, that dream turns into a nightmare? We become tongue-tied, embarrassed and imagine ourselves knocked out by superior intellect? It needn't be like that, nor need the immediate outcome of sharing our faith be our friends shunning us for ever!

Our fears usually prove unfounded. If our friends really like us, they will value what matters to us just because it matters to *us*. Furthermore, the issues raised by our faith are important, and increasingly people are realising this. Questions like 'What is life about?', 'What happens after death?', 'Do extra-terrestrials really exist?', and matters like forgiveness, justice and moral values, are still major concerns for many. People are far more tolerant of 'spiritual' approaches to life than they were even ten years ago. So perhaps we need to face our fears and remind ourselves that we do have desirable and good news to share.

How can we be ready to talk about our faith, and how can we tell when our friends are ready to listen? Fundamentally, we need to recognise that our beliefs are continually 'leak-

Friendship matters

ing out' of us all the time. The values we hold affect everything we say and do. (Thus Rosemary's neighbour was well aware that Rosemary believed in God, even though she hadn't actually said much about her faith.) This means that daily conversations will contain hooks or triggers others can utilise as cues for going further into what we believe. Obviously, if we are defensive or embarrassed when we see where the conversation might lead, our friends will pick that up (consciously or subliminally) and steer away from those kinds of issues. Conversely, there is no need to litter our talk deliberately with extra 'hot-spots' – indeed, if we do, most people will realise it and wonder about our motives for the friendship. When the quality of our friendship is strong enough, our faith will start to flow.

How can we prepare so that we are ready to give an answer for the hope that is in us? Here are some ideas.

- If you are really concerned about someone, then it is normal to want to know more about the things that matter to them. When you have discovered where your friends' interests and values are different from your own, why not seek to understand them more deeply? For instance, if a friend reads the horoscopes, perhaps you could find out what she gets out of it. Has it ever helped? Does she go through the day looking out for what has been predicted? Does she really think that life is controlled by a fate fixed by 'the stars'? There is no need to pursue these questions like a barrister – ask out of genuine interest. Almost certainly your friend will want to know why you don't read your stars, and this will give you the chance to talk about the God of love who is in charge of your life (though you may find yourself having to explain that horoscopes run counter to Christian belief, and why).

- Most non-Christians will accept that it is natural to pray

Friendship talks

for others' needs or problems. (For example, Ray did not find it at all strange that Dave should pray for his wife when she was ill.) You can use this as an opportunity to demonstrate your concern. There are a number of ways in which you might do this. You could pray without their knowing, keeping an eye on how things are progressing. Alternatively, you could let them know that you are praying for them and ask for regular updates. Or you could simply offer to pray with them when needed. You may even be part of a church prayer network, and offer to make that available. When praying with someone, it is often helpful to have ready stories to illustrate how prayer has helped others.

- Your friends will probably, at some time, express an interest in your lifestyle or beliefs. When they do, try not to be defensive. It is rarely because they want to put you down. So, if someone asks what kind of weekend you had, don't shy away from telling him what you did at church on Sunday. Perhaps you could also mention some of the positive aspects of belonging to a church family. You may even get the chance to invite the person to meet some of your Christian friends.

- Remember, too, that you don't always have to be making the first move. Perhaps *you* have been praying for something and God uses a non-Christian friend to meet your need. Be ready to express your thanks, while, at the same time, introducing the opportunity to talk about your faith. 'You really have been an answer to prayer!' 'How did you know I needed that? I've been praying about it for some time.' 'The vicar talked about something like this in the sermon last Sunday, but you've helped me to see how it can work in practice.' This kind of comment not only lets your friends know that you can (and do) involve God in the ordinary things

Friendship matters

of life; more importantly, it lets them know that you think God is already relating to and working in their lives. Imagine the repercussions of setting this thought running in someone's mind.

These are a just few suggestions as to how we can respond in ordinary situations without appearing forced or pious. Essentially, it is about making the most of everyday opportunities. The more prayerful we are, the more these opportunities seem to occur. However, one of the best preparations for friendship evangelism is to know well the story of your own journey to faith. If you haven't thought about this before, you may find it helpful to write it down. So, find a sheet of paper and a pen, and reflect on some of the following questions:

1 When did I first become aware of God as a living person?

2 What or who helped me into this awareness? The Bible, a television programme, something wonderful in nature, science, my own gifts or limitations? People at church, parents, friends, work colleagues, a preacher, a biography? Was it a mystical experience, or the answer to a prayer for help, for myself or someone else?

3 How did this happen? Was it slow or sudden? How old was I? What was going on in my life?

4 Have there been any more stages of development which had an impact? My conversion, a course of study, a new responsibility or a new stage in life?

5 What attracts me to God? What things matter most about my faith? How do these things relate to my own experience, so that they can be told as part of my story?

6 What differences has being a Christian made to my life?

Friendship talks

> Have there been times when God has guided or helped me, when I had problems or was under pressure; when I needed to give or receive forgiveness; when I faced death or illness? Have I any stories of answered prayer? What difference did particular aspects of my discipleship make?

If you are doing this in a group, talk these questions through together and give each other encouragement. One of the great things about recounting your faith story is that aspects of it which you find dull, because you have known it for so long, will really excite others.

You may want to undertake some kind of preparation course, or read books on evangelism like *Becoming a Contagious Christian* (Bill Hybels and Mark Mittelberg, Scripture Press, 1994) or *How to give away your faith* (Paul Little, InterVarsity Press, 1992). The weakness with reading is that it doesn't help us to verbalise our faith, which, like speaking a foreign language, is hard for most of us. One of the best preparation courses I know of is Evangelism Explosion which, while it does take up a lot of time (one night per week for 12–17 weeks, plus homework), works well because it combines several learning methods and practical experience. (It was Evangelism Explosion which helped Roger and Carol who, you remember, linked up with Graham and Jane.) Other simpler ways of explaining the gospel are outlined in the 'Four spiritual laws' (from Campus Crusade) and Bill Hybels' DO–DONE approach.* Something else that is particularly appropriate for the Millennium period is 'Y 2000?'. The problem with all of these is that the gospel is presented rather as a formula than the offer of an amazing friendship. They also presume a fairly substantial knowledge of the story of Jesus and, indeed, the whole Bible. However, used well and appropriately, they have a valuable contribution to make.

Friendship matters

Many people find it most helpful to be involved in groups like Alpha, which give them the opportunity to share something of their faith in a situation where people are genuinely seeking answers. When you are not on your own, the sense of responsibility and isolation which evangelism often induces is greatly lessened.

For some of us much of the time, and for all of us some of the time, it will be enough to evangelise by proxy, for example, through a video of other people's faith journeys (see The Christian Video Group series), the *Jesus* video or *Story Keepers*. Alternatively, it may be more appropriate to invite your friends to church (see the Graham and Jane story) so that they hear someone with a special gift for communication, or to introduce them to Christians who you know can help them with the faith issues that concern them.

Note

* 'Religion is spelled "D-O" because it consists of the things people do to try and gain God's forgiveness and favour ... Thankfully, Christianity is spelled differently. It is spelled "D-O-N-E", which means that what we could never do for ourselves Christ has already done for us. He lived the perfect life we could never live, and he willingly died on the cross to pay the penalty we owed for the wrongs we've done' (*Hybels and Mittelberg, Contagious Christian*, p202).

Chapter 7

DANGER!

Friendship is a fundamental necessity, especially for those who, in Michael Riddell's language, have entered Godzone.* Godzone can be any place in the world, but it is where people are searching for God. As Christians we are already in Godzone. Our friends are likely to be looking in from across the border, wondering whether to enter; or they may already have made that decision, which could well be why they find our friendship enjoyable.

Friendship is needed in Godzone because it can be lonely there: we may find ourselves particularly isolated by our commitment to the faith journey. Friendship is needed because that journey can be mighty difficult: we may require understanding, support, encouragement, practical help and spiritual guidance to keep us going. Friendship is needed because it is an essential part of life in Godzone.

However, it is because friends seem so vital, along with the special qualities attached to relationships formed in Godzone, that there are inherent dangers. We need to watch out for these, especially as they arise in the context of relational evangelism.

Negative responses

Let's suppose you have a friend you have known for a long time, even before you became a Christian. You enjoy doing things together. You have honest discussions on all kinds of matters, like the politics of Northern Ireland, why people spend money on the lottery, coping with the ups and downs of family life, worries about global warming or genetic engineering, why Manchester United are (or are *not*) the greatest team in the Premier League, and what you think of digital television. You are also fairly comfortable talking to her about what you do at church, and have been hinting for ages that there's more to it than religion. Your friend may even be asking questions about what you believe. You sense that your prayers, and those of your prayer partners, are being answered. Soon you hope to invite your friend to an Alpha meal or to introduce her to someone you think might help her to make that decision to become a Christian.

Then, either abruptly or like a misty summer drizzle, the atmosphere changes. Your friend seems cool towards you, giving the impression that she has totally gone off you. She makes comments about how dull you are now; how this Christianity, far from making you better or happier, seems to have made you more judgemental and less fun. Little by little, you sense that she is hiding things from you that before she would have shared. Imperceptibly, the warmth and flexibility in the relationship, which you thought you had both valued, dissolves. Far from looking towards the time her becoming a Christian seemed inevitable, you realise that, actually, the road your friend is travelling has turned away from yours.

You could react in a number of ways. You could reject your friend, get very depressed or belittle yourself for having made a mess of it. You may even suspect that she is right – you *were* better off before you became a Christian and took a trip out of the real world! However, none of these responses are likely to be appropriate for what has actually gone wrong. Instead, it may be more helpful to pause, sit down and do some spiritual stock-taking. Reflecting on the following questions may get you started.

Danger!

1 Is there any validity in the negative messages you are getting? If there might be, why not ask your friend how you can be a better friend to her? By doing this, you are showing that you value her and want the friendship to continue.

2 Check whether or not you are getting the right message. It can be illuminating to ask, 'This is what I hear you saying. Is this what you really mean?' If there is any doubt, you could then go on to explore whether the problems are more to do with your friend's feelings than with the actual relationship. Obviously care is needed here, as you could come across as patronising or prying, which will only drive her further away.

3 Why not tell your friend how much and in what ways you value her? She may well be thinking that you are itching to drop her now that you have this bunch of Christian friends to whom you seem to give so much time. She may be thinking that she will only be good enough for you when she submits to this Christian stuff, or indeed that she will never be good enough. If the Holy Spirit is working in her, in response to your prayers, she may be feeling uncomfortable or guilty about things in her life which your new faith has brought to the fore. She may be going through a time of loss: you have something she cannot share; your friendship isn't the same and never will be. She may be on the verge of making a commitment, and be going through the turmoil of changing attitudes and priorities that this involves.

4 If your friend is afraid of being trapped into becoming a Christian because of her long-standing relationship with you, you can allay her fears in two ways. First, be sure to explain (maybe 'hint' is a better word) that one of the essential things about meeting with Jesus is that it has to be a free choice; let her know that you would never abuse your friendship; if ever she feels that you are, she must tell you. Second, give her some space, assuring her that you will miss her company and are not going to reject her. Great sensitivity is required here, as your 'stepping back' may seem like evidence that you are looking for a way out of the friendship; so offer plenty of reassurance.

5 With any of the above approaches, it is essential to pray about the relationship – and I mean real honest prayer, telling God how you feel (fed up, angry, totally despondent, bemused) and asking him what to do and when. The depth of your prayers will depend on how strong is your desire to see your friend fall into the arms of Christ and find new life. It is easy, when a relationship is in trouble, to be so concerned about preserving it that we forget *why* it matters so much.

Close encounters of a troublesome kind

As we have seen, our friendships can hit a difficult patch just as we seem to be making progress. One obvious reason for this is that Satan doesn't want them to work out well for God's kingdom, so if he can't break them up he will try blowing them out of the water altogether. Thus, it is less common, but nevertheless frequent enough to be worth noting, that rather than friendships breaking up they blossom too rapidly!

Again it is not hard to see why. The ability to form good quality friendships often grows with our Christian maturity. If we are truly seeking to live the Christian way and to submit ourselves to God's claims on us, we are likely to become even more desirable as friends to those around us. The quality of Jesus' friendship is incomparable. No one is more loving, sensitive, committed, helpful, honest but gentle, self-giving, alert to the joys of the universe and willing to share them. No one is more fun to be with and more dependable to get you out of any mess. He is wise beyond estimation, with a great sense of humour, too. We can trust him with any murky secret, but this doesn't stop him from loving us. If it is true that we become like those who love us and whom we love, then if we are Christians we should be growing, bit by bit, more like Jesus. As the Holy Spirit pours his love into our hearts, this love will flow from us more fully, and we will grow in our capacity to form relationships that are deeper and closer than usual.

Great, we think, *my friend is moving towards the magic moment of Christian decision. Praise you, Lord. Let there be still more.*

Great, Satan thinks, *they are sailing into my trap...*

The friendship can over-blow in several ways. The most blatant (and therefore the most infrequent) is that it develops into a dangerous liaison that results in an emptying of the Christian's testimony. The non-Christian friend may enjoy the closeness of the relationship without understanding the implications of the other's commitment to Christ, with damaging consequences. Thus the Christian may find himself involved in a sexual relationship or some other activity contrary to his principles; or he may panic because he sees where the relationship is going, and thinks that he had better get out before 'the cub becomes the beast' and is too big to handle. Another, more likely outcome is that one or other party is unable or unwilling to give the time and the commitment necessary for the friendship to prosper. And finally, the jealousy or disapproval of a third party may set off a series of seismic disturbances which, in the end, destroy the relationship.

How can we avoid these pitfalls? The main thing is not to panic but to be honest and prayerful, allowing God to work in the situation. Right from the start, thank him for what he is doing and ask him to help you find a way out of the relationship's problems which is honouring to Jesus as well as fruitful in terms of evangelism.

To gain a more objective understanding of what is happening, it is worth sharing your concerns with another Christian who can pray for you, help you see where God is leading you, and lend a listening ear when the difficulties threaten to overwhelm you. He or she might also become involved in the relationship, thus broadening the non-Christian's experience of Christian people. However, the person you choose must be mature enough in the faith to cope with the relationship's problems and be discreet about them. Imagine how your friend would feel if she discovered that you had been talking about her to someone else and that you saw her as a problem.

Suitable candidates for your confidant include your home-group leader, the chairman of the evangelism committee, someone who nurtured you, your pastor. Perhaps you could make a list and pray about the people on it, asking God who he has in mind, always being ready for him to bring someone you hadn't thought of into the selection process. Then prioritise your list and approach them in that order, until you find someone who is able to give you time. Explain that you have something important, even exciting, that you want to talk through with them. Exciting? It probably doesn't seem like that to you now because the friendship is a problem. Nevertheless, it *is* exciting, because it shows that you are making real progress in your capacity to build relationships, in the quality of the friendship you are offering, and in giving others the opportunity to experience valid Christian commitment.

Before meeting up with your confidant, you may find that it helps to write your concerns down. Think about your friendship and how long you have been consciously seeking to bring your friend to Jesus. Where might it all go wrong? How does it 'feel' to you? The value of doing this is that it ensures that you don't forget anything, and it may bolster your confidence so that you don't leave out issues because they seem too trivial or too dangerous to mention. Equally, it should help you avoid turning the session into a time of gossip or complaint. It is important, as you work on this together, to remember that your non-Christian friend *is* your friend. When you have talked and prayed this all through with your confidant, agree a plan of action which includes a commitment from him or her to go on praying for you. Then arrange future meetings so that you both keep track of your progress.

As if relationships developing too rapidly were not enough, the opposite may also occur. Consciously or otherwise, your friend may start testing the relationship – picking quarrels, letting you down, talking behind your back, making uncharacteristic demands on you. Gradually, you become aware that this is not just an odd occurrence – a pattern is developing. You may find yourself wondering, 'What have I done to deserve this!?' However, in doing this your friend may be trying to discover several things. Are you serious about her as a person, or is she merely a target for your Christian sales pitch? More profoundly, she may be trying to find out if what you say about Christianity works. Is love for keeps? Is forgiveness a reality? How much does she really mean to you? She may even be considering Christ's offer of friendship and the only way she can test Jesus' claim is to try it out on his ambassador – you!

Once we recognise what is going on and why, we can begin to see how we might respond. Again, thank God for the positive: these kinds of problems mean that your friend is nearer the kingdom. Then ask the Holy Spirit to help you to keep things in proportion, to know what to say and what not to say, especially when you are hurting, and to be faithful in loving your friend. Focus on what you like about her and about the friendship, and why. Fixing your eyes on the positive will help you get through the negative (Hebrews 12:2).

In the end, it may be that you will have to be more direct and share what you are feeling with your friend. A loving rather than confrontational approach is best. Has she noticed that the friendship is going through a difficult patch? Does she have any sense as to why this might be? Let her know your thoughts and ask for her comments. Again, it is helpful to talk the situation through beforehand with a Christian you can trust, asking for insight and the commitment to pray while you work through the issues with your non-Christian friend.

When friendship fails

Always, we have to put our commitment to Christ before our commitment to the friendship. Sometimes (more rarely than we might fear), this will mean we have to walk away from it. We may need to do this:

- If the relationship can only continue if we compromise our faith, eg it becomes sexual or involves breaking the law.

- If our friendship is getting out of control and we will be trapped by it.

- If it is succeeding in destroying our faith.

Please note that I say walk away from the friendship and not from the friend. Be careful to avoid sending the message that you are rejecting her as a person. Simply say that, for the time being, you both need a break from each other. It may be possible to keep the door open for the relationship to be renewed at a later date – in, say, a couple of months – though this will depend on the reasons for the split. Try to use the separation as an opportunity to express appreciation for the good things you have shared together, to thank your friend for her part in it and to wish her well.

More frequently, it is your friend who wants to walk away from you, perhaps because of your faith. Obviously, when this happens, you need to check that it is not because you *are* being pompous or defensive. If you do have to take responsibility for damaging the relationship, seek your friend's forgiveness and, again, leave the way open for a renewal of the friendship.

It may be, however, that what your friend is rejecting is Jesus. In this case, you may need to be ready just to let it happen. Remember, Jesus let people go (Mark 10:22). And, though we may love our friends, we should love Christ more: we certainly cannot deny him and all that he stands for.

For many Christians, the fear of rejection is imprisoning, hindering them from making any attempt to share their faith. It is not surprising, since rejection is very painful. But such rejection is very rare. When a friend turns down an offer or invitation, do not immediately jump to the conclusion that it is a major rejection of you: there could be all kinds of reasons.

However a friendship comes to an end, there will be pain and you will need help to cope from other Christians. However it ends, remember that God has not finished yet with either you or your friend. Continue to pray that God will work in your friend's life. Surrendering someone to God is an important spiritual and psychological step: otherwise, you may continue to grieve or carry guilt inappropriately, and prevent God from doing new things in both your lives. If your friend forms a new relationship with another Christian, then, however hard it may be, thank God for this answer to your prayers. You may feel like a failure, but you should not. All you have done is try to love someone into the kingdom. Knowing that you have lost the joy of a friendship because of your commitment to Christ will not necessarily stop these kinds of feelings, but don't let them stop you from trying again.

Friendship matters

For further reflection

Spend some time reviewing your friendships. You may find the following questions helpful. If you belong to a group, work through them together.

1 Is my friendship developing or declining? (Factors to consider might include openness in conversation, empathy, time spent together, enjoyment, how does it feel.)

2 When was the last time I had opportunity to share something about my faith with my friend (by word, by deed)?

3 Am I maintaining my commitment to pray for my friend? Do I have a sense of what God's next step for him/her is? When did I last note an answer to my prayers for my friend? Did I thank God for it?

4 Have I been able to introduce my friend to other Christians? (If you are going through these questions with a group, come up with some practical ways to help one another do this.)

5 Are there any signs that indicate an increase or decrease in my friend's interest in the Good News or in Christian matters? (Factors to consider include asking questions, making comments, interest in coming to Christian events, books, videos.)

Having reflected on your friendships, take time to thank God for any progress you have made, asking him for wisdom to deal with any difficulties. Commit yourself again to sharing the Good News with your friend.

Note
* Michael Riddell, *Godzone: A Traveller's Guide*, Lion Publishing, 1992.

Chapter 8

ON THE WAY

User-friendly recap

Chapters 2, 3 and 4 looked at specific examples of friendship evangelism, whether they were real-life stories, material collated for case studies or biblical examples.

Chapters 5 and 6 discussed principles, although still with real-life application. Chapter 5 showed us how we might improve our effectiveness as friends by increasing our availability. We considered how we might recognise the people God wants us to form friendships with and how we might improve the quality of the friendship we offer. We took a brief look at how forming friendships is very much a part of being a Christian, underlining the fact that our friendship must have integrity and not merely be a means to an end. Chapter 6 suggested ways in which we could improve our ability to talk naturally and clearly about our beliefs within the relational context.

Chapter 7 explored some of the various reactions we might expect, ranging from the relationship becoming too intimate too quickly, to handling anger and rejection. We considered how and why these reactions happen, but also suggested coping strategies.

Hopefully, by now you are well on the way to being excited about the possibility of sharing the reality of Jesus with your friends, as an inevitable and desirable part of friendship. If we want to share our experiences, interests, memories and activities, how can we not want to release into our friendship all that Jesus and belonging to his people means to us? If we enjoy introducing our friends to each other, why do we hesitate to introduce someone to Jesus?

Perhaps you have simply got on with the job. You may be the outgoing, friendly type who finds friendship evangelism easy and wonders why we need books on the subject! You may be a relatively new Christian who hasn't yet picked up the bad habits and blind spots of those who have been in the faith longer. If so, bear with me. This final chapter is probably more geared towards encouraging those of us who are finding it hard to get started. However, it may even help if you are ahead of the game!

Getting started

Providing the time, support, love and help that someone may need, as they move towards making a decision about Jesus, will require a lot from us. It is probably impossible to give serious attention to more than two or three at a time, so we need to be realistic and concentrate our energies on a few people. This does not mean we forget to pray for our other friends, or to share our faith as and when the opportunity arises.

You may find it helpful to make a list of all your friends and acquaintances, and spend time praying for each name, thanking God for them and the things you value in them. Then consider the following questions: while they do not guarantee that you will find the right people to focus on, they offer useful pointers.

- Are there any indications that your friends are becoming more aware of spiritual matters or even of the Christian faith?

- Is there a sense that your friendship is growing?

- Are there crises in their lives (including significant positive changes) which appear to give you a special opportunity?

- Do you have a special concern to see any of them become Christians soon?

- Do you find that your mind and heart keep returning to particular individuals? (It may be that a past friend, with whom you don't have an active friendship at the moment, keeps popping into your head.)

- Do you keep meeting one of your friends more than normal, or have openings to pray with or for him/her?

With these questions in mind, narrow your list of potential friends down to two or three. Then, prayerfully, ask God to show you how he is working in their lives. Make it clear to him that you are willing to share your life with these people, so that they can be blessed by him and become available to Christ. In turn, God may give you a personal conviction about someone. As you sense, increasingly, that a particular person is the right one for you to focus on, commit yourself to pray for her daily, bringing her lovingly before God, telling him that you want to see her become part of his kingdom. Ask him to give you opportunities to explore further the rightness of your growing conviction. When you become certain, promise him that you will stick with the relationship until he releases you. You may find seeds of doubt in your mind that you have chosen in line with God's will. A useful counter-strategy is to decide that these people will do until God shows you otherwise.

Once you have settled on 'Who', the next step is to give some consideration as to 'How'. If you are a very spontaneous kind of person, this may seem false and manipulative to you. Nevertheless, take from this section those ideas which seem practical and with which you feel most comfortable.

1. Build up a picture of where the person is spiritually. What do you know about their previous contacts with and experience of Christians, the church or the Bible? Have they ever thought about the big questions of life, such as 'Where do we come from? Why are we here? What happens after death?' What are their views on issues like justice, forgiveness, freedom and fate, honesty? Have they had / do they have contact with other spiritual belief systems or practices, eg another religion, horoscopes, the occult? What would it be interesting or helpful for them to know about the Christian view on these things? Look for opportunities to find out.

2. As you refine your picture, begin to work out what would bring them nearer to Christ, eg breaking with things that are a hindrance, growing in their understanding of the Christian faith. Pray for these to happen and look for opportunities to help them happen. Don't fall into the trap of thinking that changes will only occur if you provide the opportunity, or even worse, engineer the outcome. God is able to do most things without us, but he does love to involve us in the process. As you see progress, it is often better not to underline this fact to your friend but, rather, to thank God for what he is doing.

3. Are there aspects of your life which are preventing your friend from coming into relationship with Christ? Start to work out with God how the necessary changes in you can come about. Obviously, I do not mean allowing friends to manipulate you into becoming someone you are not or doing things that are out of character; instead, recognise

that our commitment to see our friends come into the kingdom may well have a high, even invasive, price tag.

4 Consider specific activities that may help the friendship to progress, and how and when they might happen, then pray towards them. While it would be wrong to set a timetable for the development of a friendship, there is nothing wrong in setting ourselves a timetable for actions that are our responsibility to take.

5 Make up your mind to enjoy your relationships and all that goes with them. We are not wanting to detract from the wonder of friendship, but to add to it by bringing Christ more fully into the circle.

Praying

At various points through this book, the importance of prayer has been noted as an essential ingredient in friendship evangelism. There is no doubt, both biblically and experientially, that prayer is vital. A real challenge for each of us is how to sustain insightful and effective prayer. Some people will find it simpler to rely on intuition and pray for people as they happen to come to mind. Others will prefer more organised prayer activities, such as prayer triplets or keeping a list in their diary or Bible. (Prayer Triplet cards are available from the Evangelical Alliance, 186 Kennington Park Road, London SE11 4BT; tel 0171 207 2100.) Still others will find small groups like Community Prayer Cells a good stimulus for consistent prayer, building friendships and receiving support. (A video and workbook on Community Prayer Cells are available from CPAS, Athena Drive, Tachbrook Park, Warwick CV34 6NG.) There is no right or wrong method.

As well as praying for our friends, it is also good to pray for our friends' families and contacts, so that, spiritually speaking, we are preparing the way for them. Then, when our friends come to faith, they already have people who are being prepared through prayer to receive God's love.

Praying for friends

We are almost at the end of our exploration of friendship evangelism (though there are other books in this series, see page 4). However, important and helpful as books are, progress should not be measured by how many books you get through on a subject, but whether or not you are getting on in sharing the Good News of Jesus with your friends. Friendship evangelism really works. God wants it to work. The fact that you have come so far with this book shows that *you* want it to work. Getting started will be the hardest bit, so – if you have not already done so – as you close this book, open your heart to God. Tell him of your desire to share his love and his Son with your friends. Let him excite you about the wonderful partnership you have entered into with him. Dream of the joy your friends will discover as it dawns on them why they were born, where they are going and how Jesus' friendship can unite you. You may like to use the following prayer to help you:

Dear Father God,

Thank you that you sent Jesus to die for my sins and brought him back from death to be my eternal friend. Thank you for all the love, help and hope I have received through Jesus.

Thank you too, for all my other friends, for the enrichment, fun and strength we gain from each other. Lord, I especially thank you for *(name)*.

I long for *(name)* to know you, as I know you, to love you as I love you, to serve you as I long to serve you. I offer you my friendship with *(name)* so that you can use me to help them discover the life and wonder of Jesus. You know my anxieties, help me with them. You know my hopes, bring

On the way

them to fulfilment in your time. Keep me faithful in prayer, consistent in my relationship and always loving.

Through Jesus Christ I pray. Amen.

A start chart

```
Name ......................................
Initial prayer ..............................
..........................................
..........................................
..........................................
..........................................
..........................................
Next contact ...............................
Further prayers ............................
..........................................
..........................................
..........................................
..........................................
..........................................
..........................................
Progress (Events, dates, signs of progress) ........
..........................................
..........................................
..........................................
..........................................
..........................................
..........................................
..........................................
..........................................
..........................................
..........................................
```

Other titles in the 'Relating Good News' series

Wake up to Work: Friendship and Faith in the Workplace, Geoff Shattock.

Man to Man: Friendship and Faith, Steven Croft.

Sharing the Salt: Making Friends with Sikhs, Muslims and Hindus, Ida Glaser and Shaylesh Raja.